Sniggles, Squirrels, and Chicken Pox

By "Miss Jackie" Weissman

© 1984 by Jackie Weissman

Second printing

ISBN 939514 - 06 - 0

Published by MISS JACKIE MUSIC COMPANY, 10001 El Monte, Overland Park, Kansas 66207

All rights reserved. No part of this publication may be reproduced, stored in a retrieval system or transmitted in any form or by any means, electronic, mechanical, photocopying, recording, or otherwise, without the prior written permission of the publisher. Printed in the United States of America.

Cover design by Cynthia Fowler

Editor: Jerry Maloney

Distributed by Gryphon House
3706 Otis Street
P.O. Box 211
Mt. Rainier, Maryland 20822

FROM THE AUTHOR

Miss Jackie

   MOST of the songs in "Sniggles, Squirrels, and Chicken Pox" were originally written for *The Instructor* magazine, the prestigious magazine for teachers. The other songs, notably "The Sniggle Song" and "No, No, No," were developed during the classes I conduct for parents and children in my course, "Music, Mom, Dad, and Me."

WE HAD received numerous requests for a collection of these songs, and this book is a response to those requests.

THE MUSIC can be used in a classroom setting, in the home, for youth groups, camps, preschools, or nurseries. There are suggested activities that accompany each song.

ALL OF the songs are open-ended. That is, they allow for your own creativity to extend the song.

THE ACTIVITIES will develop listening, language, cognitive and motor skills which, in turn, develop self concept.

SING these songs with your children. Laugh, pretend, run, jump, hug, and enjoy!!

TABLE OF CONTENTS

SEPTEMBER

Sing a Song of September 6
Roses Are Red 8
Aloha 9
How to Be a Good Citizen 10

OCTOBER

Furry Squirrel 12
Black Cat 14
Halloween 15
Wee Willie Winkle 16

NOVEMBER

Read Read Books Books 18
Animals Are My Friends 19
Hanukah 20
Turkey Talk 21

DECEMBER

Give 22
Little Betty Blue 24
The Sniggle Song 25
Nine Little Reindeer 26

JANUARY

Going out to Play 28
No, No, No, ... 29
Sing About Martin 30
Ride, Sally, Ride 32

FEBRUARY

Hooray for Mr. Lincoln 34
Look Ma, No Cavities 36
Groundhog 38
United 40

MARCH

Goodbye Winter, Hello Spring... 42
King of the Jungle 44
Easter Bunny 46
Diddle, Diddle, Dumpling 48

APRIL

Whistling Cowhand 50
Baby Moses 51
Baby Bear's Chicken Pox 52
Water in the Rain Clouds 53

MAY

Today Is May... 54
Conversation with a Tree 55
Worms 56
Old Mother Hubbard 58

JUNE

Peter Piper... 60
Little Miss Muffet 61
Rain 62
Hey Diddle, Diddle 63
Index by First Lines 64
About Miss Jackie 66

SING A SONG OF SEPTEMBER

Words and Music by
"Miss Jackie" Weissman

Sing a song, sing a song of Sep-tem-ber.
Sing a song of the fal-ling leaves.
Sing a 1. friends and school and winds so cool.
       2. birds and squir-rels and boys and girls.
Sing a song of Sep-tem-ber. Sing a-bout Sep-tem-ber.
Sing a sweet Sep-tem-ber song.

© 1981

ACTIVITIES

THIS song has a flowing, lilting feeling and suggests movement. Use a triangle or a bell to accompany the song and have the children dance, jump, hop, or skip as you sing the song.

MAKE a list of all the things associated with September and substitute those words in the two rhyming lines. Your words do not have to rhyme. The song is open-ended, and its purpose is to create a good feeling about September.

YOU CAN also sing the song about October, November, and December by making up the appropriate words. For example: "Sing of witches and goblins and Halloween," or "Sing of Santa and presents and Christmas trees."

RELATED ACTIVITIES

TAKE a nature walk and observe September—the changing color of the leaves, the feel of the wind, the intensity of the sun.

ASK THE children to bring in leaves. Study the differences in shape, size, and design.

THIS is a good song for introducing the sound of "S." Pick out all the words in the song that start with "S." Discuss the meaning of the words.

PLAY this game: Each time the children hear the sound of "S," they raise their hands, wiggle a finger, or shake their foot.

INSTEAD of "Sing a Song," why not "Dance a Song," "Jump a Song," or "Hop a Song"? Or any other rhythm motor movement that your children can do.

ROSES ARE RED

Adapted words and original music by "Miss Jackie" Weissman

Roses are red. Violets are blue. Sugar is sweet and so are you. Sugar is sweet and so are you.

©1983

THIS song presents many opportunities to help children develop their natural creativity, make them aware of their own environment, and practice rhyming. Here are some ideas:

1. CHANGE the colors: Roses are green, violets are black. Then change the rhyme: Teacher is fun, duckies go quack. See if the children can make some rhymes.

2. SENSORY development: What else is sweet? Sour? Spicy? Change the words to fit the discussion: Apples are sweet, vinegar is sour.

3. WHAT other songs have colors in them? "Yellow Submarine," "A Dog Named Blue," "Yellowbird."

4. PLAY a color game. Assemble a group of pre-cut matching shapes of different colors. Have the children sing the song. When they come to red, have them pick out the shapes that are red. Then blue, etc.

5. FIND other songs about flowers.

ALOHA

Words and Music by
"Miss Jackie" Weissman

© 1978

OUR 50th state is a very beautiful and special place. It has its own music, folklore, dancing and language.

THE WORD "Aloha" is fun to say and lovely to listen to.

DISCUSS with the children how you can greet someone with "Aloha" and how you can say good-bye with "Aloha." Shake hands, wave in different ways, hug and embrace, etc. As you sing the song, let the children use the actions they have chosen with the word "Aloha."

THIS song is nice to sing while standing in a circle. All of the children can see each other and it adds for a more pleasureful experience.

ON THE interlude part, the children can sway their bodies to the music. If you know someone who can teach "hula" steps, this would be the perfect place to do the steps.

PICTURES and other visuals would be very helpful in the children's understanding of Hawaii.

HOW TO BE A GOOD CITIZEN

Words and Music by
"Miss Jackie" Weissman

1. Picking the trash up off the street,
Off the street, off the street.
Picking the trash up off the street,
That's how to be a good citizen.

2. Obeying rules at school each day,
School each day, school each day.
Obeying rules at school each day,
That's how to be a good citizen.

What can I do? Something that really matters?
How can I help To make the world a little better?

© 1982

ACTIVITIES

THIS song provides an opportunity for talking and singing about good citizenship. This concept is understandable to young children if it is presented at their own level. Being proud of your school, your family, or your community is within a child's cognitive grasp.

ASK QUESTIONS such as: "What makes you proud of your school?" Use the answers to substitute for the words in the song. For example:

> Picking the toys up off the floor, off the floor, off the floor.
> Hanging the pictures on the wall, on the wall, on the wall.

TALK about some of the good citizens in the community. Who keeps the community safe, clean, and interesting? Who takes care of the family, the school, the home? Find pictures of these good citizens and make up words to go with the song.

MAKE a list of good citizenship ideas. Assign one thing to each student. Make a chart and, as these tasks are completed, sing the song using the compiled ideas.

RHYTHM—Accompany the song with tambourines, sand blocks, and rhythm sticks. The words that repeat themselves provide an opportunity for solo singing or solo playing of a rhythm instrument.

DRAW pictures of good citizenship ideas. Take a walk and pick up litter. Talk about helping an elderly person across the street.

FURRY SQUIRREL

ACTIVITIES

FURRY, bushy, and scamper are good vocabulary words. Discuss what is furry, what is bushy. How do you scamper? Use visual, tactile and movement experiences to help the children understand the words better.

A GOOD discussion question is: "Why do squirrels look for nuts?"

THE ENTIRE song is wonderful for creative dramatics. After the word "nuts" at the end of the first section, the children have a tendency to repeat "nuts, nuts, nuts." This could be accompanied with rhythm instruments.

THE SECOND part of the song identifies body parts. The children could touch the body parts as they sing.

RELATED ACTIVITIES

NATURE WALK—Take the class for a walk outdoors. Look for squirrels and acorns. Discuss how the squirrels climb, how they scamper, how they hold nuts in their paws.

GAME—*Squirrels in the Trees* is a very popular game for young children. Groups of two or three children hold hands to form the trees. One child acts as the squirrel in each tree, and one child is a squirrel without a tree. The treeless squirrel says, "Squirrels, scamper to find nuts." Kids run around the trees until the command comes, "Squirrels, go inside a tree." Each child goes inside a tree and the one without a tree gets to give the commands next time.

COGNITIVE SKILL—Bring several kinds of nuts to class. Have the children sort them according to size, color, and shape. Talk about the names of the nuts, how they feel, and then, of course, eat them. Shelling peanuts is a good exercise in motor development.

FUN—Have the children try to balance nuts on their noses, on their toes, on their heads.

THE BLACK CAT

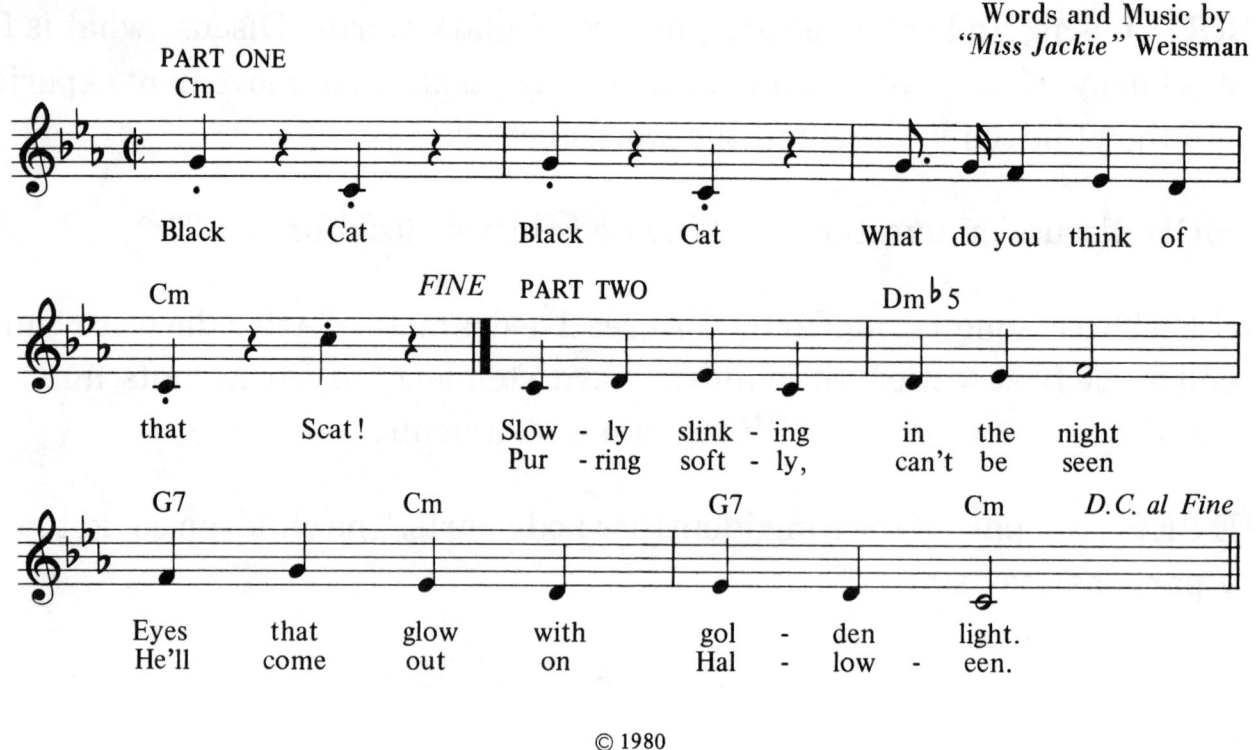

Words and Music by
"Miss Jackie" Weissman

© 1980

THIS song has two parts. In the first part, the words stay the same. In the second part, the words change. You can make up some of your own words in part two, or you can make up some of the words and let the children fill in the rhyme.

IT'S FUN to sing the first part in a very soft voice until you come to the word "Scat." Have the children clap their hands and sing "Scat!" in a GREAT BIG voice.

LISTENING SKILLS—Pick three words about Halloween. For example: witch, black cat, pumpkin. Make up a story and use these words. The children listen for the words and make the appropriate sound each time they hear the words.

DISCRIMINATION—Draw two similar black cats but with slight differences. For example, the tails could be on different sides or curved differently. They could have differently shaped eyes, different smiles, etc. Have the children discover the differences. You could draw the cats on cards and have the children sort the cards into the different categories.

FUN—Be a black cat for the day. Have the children move like black cats.

HALLOWEEN

Words and Music by
"Miss Jackie" Weissman

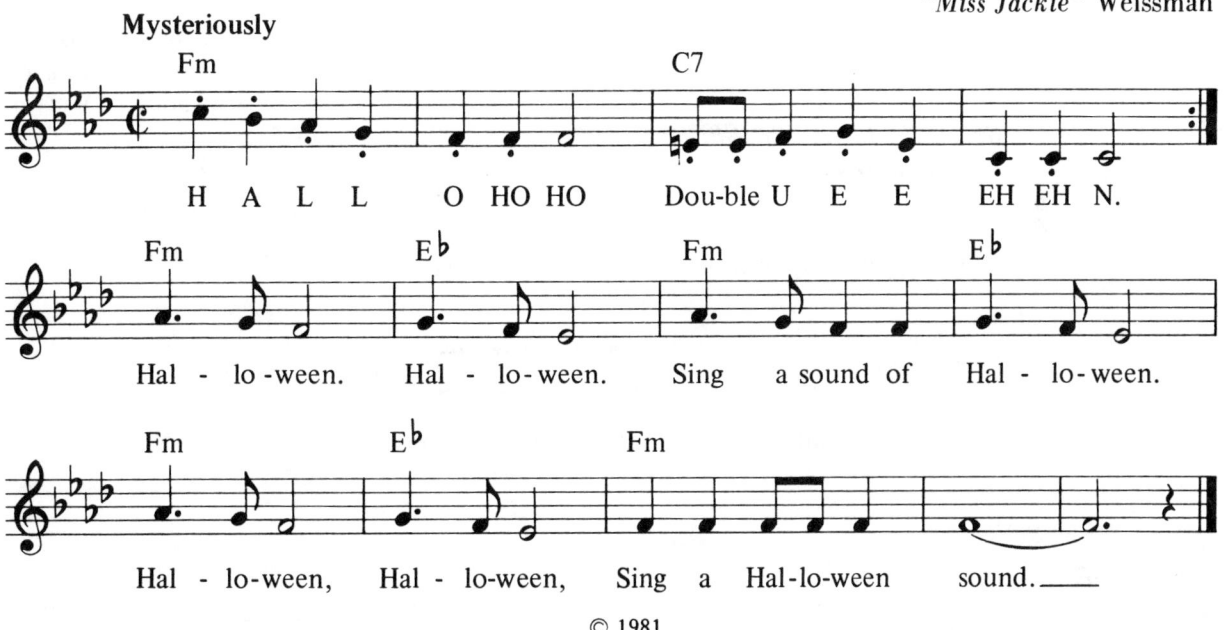

© 1981

WHAT are all the different sounds you hear at Halloween time? Sing the song and then make a Halloween sound. You can also sing the song in all kinds of spooky voices—a witch's voice, a black cat's voice, a ghost's voice, a monster's voice.

THE SONG also teaches the children to spell the word "Halloween."

GAME—One child is chosen to make the Halloween sound at the end of the song. The other children have to guess what the sound is. Whoever guesses first gets to make the next sound.

STORY—Tell the children a story about Halloween. Assign certain sounds to go with certain words. Whenever the children hear the word, they make the appropriate sound.

LISTENING SKILLS—Record Halloween sounds on a tape recorder. Have pictures ready that go with the sounds (black cat, witch). Play the recording and have the children identify the sound by finding the correct picture.

CLASSIFICATION—Classify all the different kinds of sounds. There are high sounds, low sounds, scary sounds, loud sounds, soft sounds, etc. See how many categories of sound the children can name. Then try to name different things that fit into the categories. Try to make the sounds.

WEE WILLIE WINKIE

Adapted words
and original music by
"Miss Jackie" Weissman

SPOKEN IN A WHISPER:

Ev-ery bo-dy qui-et. Don't make a peep.
Shh   Shh   Act like you're a-sleep.

THEN SING:

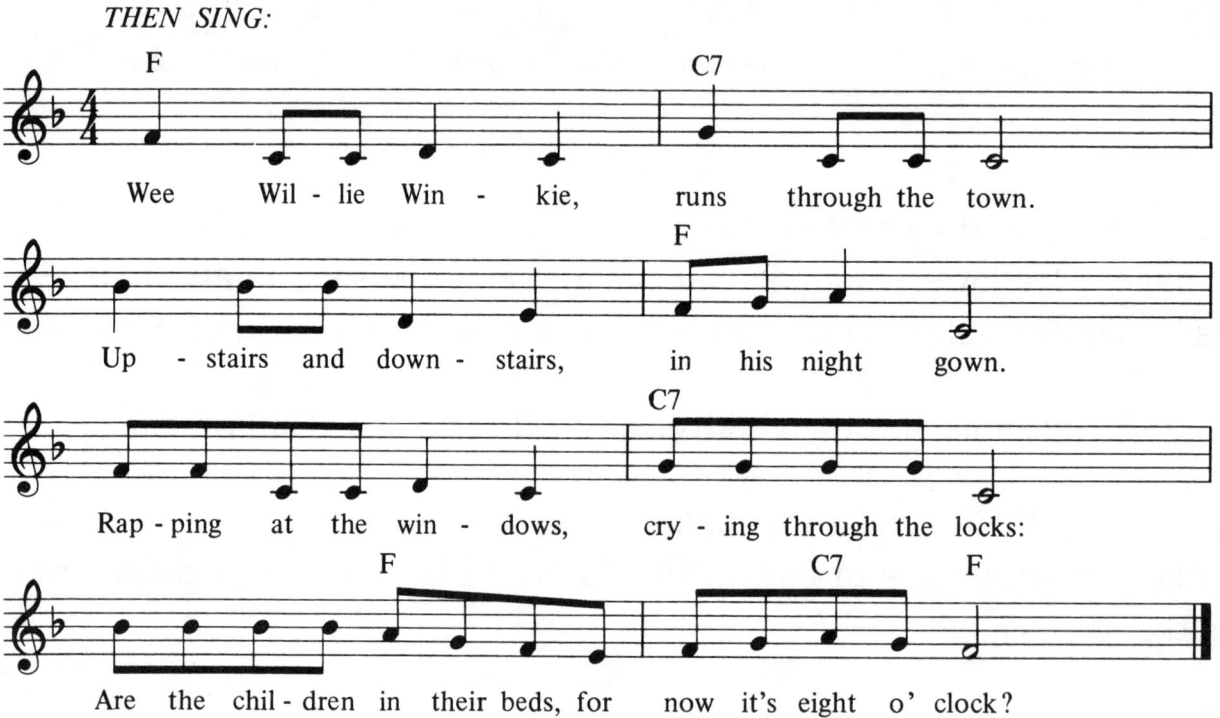

Wee Wil-lie Win-kie, runs through the town.
Up-stairs and down-stairs, in his night gown.
Rap-ping at the win-dows, cry-ing through the locks:
Are the chil-dren in their beds, for now it's eight o' clock?

© 1982

ACTIVITIES

CHILDREN sometimes like to pretend they're sleeping when their parents look into their rooms. The whisper part of this song creates suspense for singing the rest of the song. Perhaps the class could be divided into two groups: One group sings the whisper part, the other group sings the rest of the song.

TIME—This is a good song for working on time. Some schools have clocks with movable hands. The teacher sets the time and the children fill in the correct time when they sing the last line of the song.

VOCABULARY—Talk about the meaning of the words. What does "crying through the locks" mean? "Crying" doesn't always mean weeping. Sometimes it can mean calling or yelling. "Rapping at the windows" could be substituted with other expressions.

CREATIVE DRAMATICS—The last line in which Wee Willie Winkle speaks can be spoken in many different voices, giving lots of children a chance to be Wee Willie. Have the children sing the last in different ways—happy, sad, angry, silly, etc. Say the line very slowly, then very quickly, very high, then very low.

PARENT PROGRAM—Have one group of the children sing the song. Have the rest of the class act out the song. Let the groups switch roles.

READ READ BOOKS BOOKS

Words and Music by
"Miss Jackie" Weissman

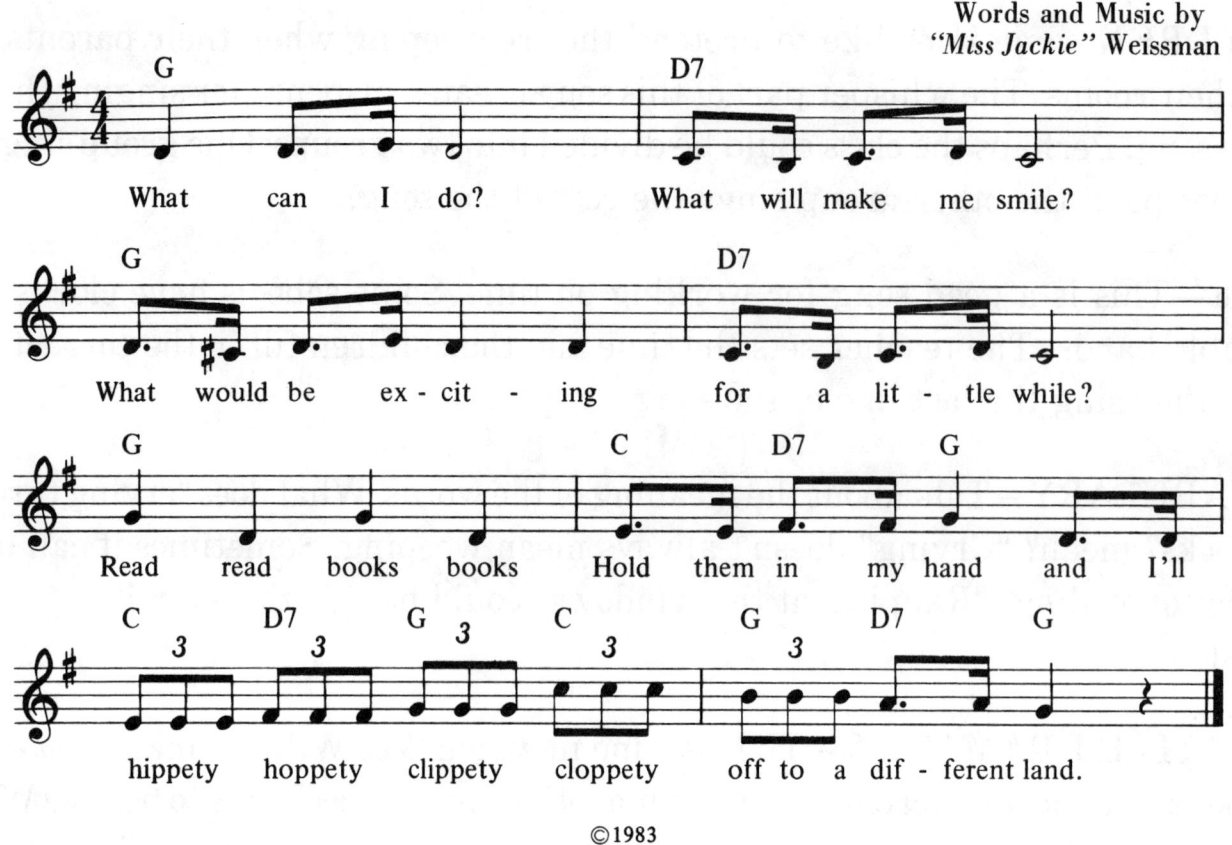

©1983

THIS song will help young children to think about books, motivate them to read books, and realize how wonderful books are. The idea is to draw vocabulary from the children and insert it into the song.

THE WORDS to the song stay the same except "hold them in my hand" and "off to a different land." When you come to these words, ask the children to substitute their own words. For example, here's a verse made up by a four-year-old:

> Read Read Books Books
> Monsters eating grass
> Hippety, hoppety, clippety, cloppety
> Right into the water.

THE WORDS "hippety, hoppety, clippety, cloppety" are fun to sing and children love to repeat them. It's also fun to tap fingers and toes to the rhythm of the words.

THE WORDS DON'T HAVE TO RHYME!!

ANIMALS ARE MY FRIENDS

Words and Music by
"Miss Jackie" Weissman

©1984

THE SONG "Animals Are My Friends" has a dual purpose. First, it puts children in touch with their environment. Second, it gives them a chance to rhyme words for reading improvement.

A DISCUSSION about the animals around us will lead to conversations about pets, the zoo, and farm animals. Talking about taking care of animals, responsibilty to animals, will interest the children very much. The words in the song "Animals Are My Friends" will help them internalize the need to care for animals.

THE BRIDGE of the song is open-ended so that the children can use their imagination and rhyme other words. For example, a giraffe can make you laugh, a snake can help you bake, etc.

THE MOST important concept to get across is that we share this world with lots of other creatures and we must be aware that animals need to be treated kindly.

HANUKAH

Words and Music by
"Miss Jackie" Weissman

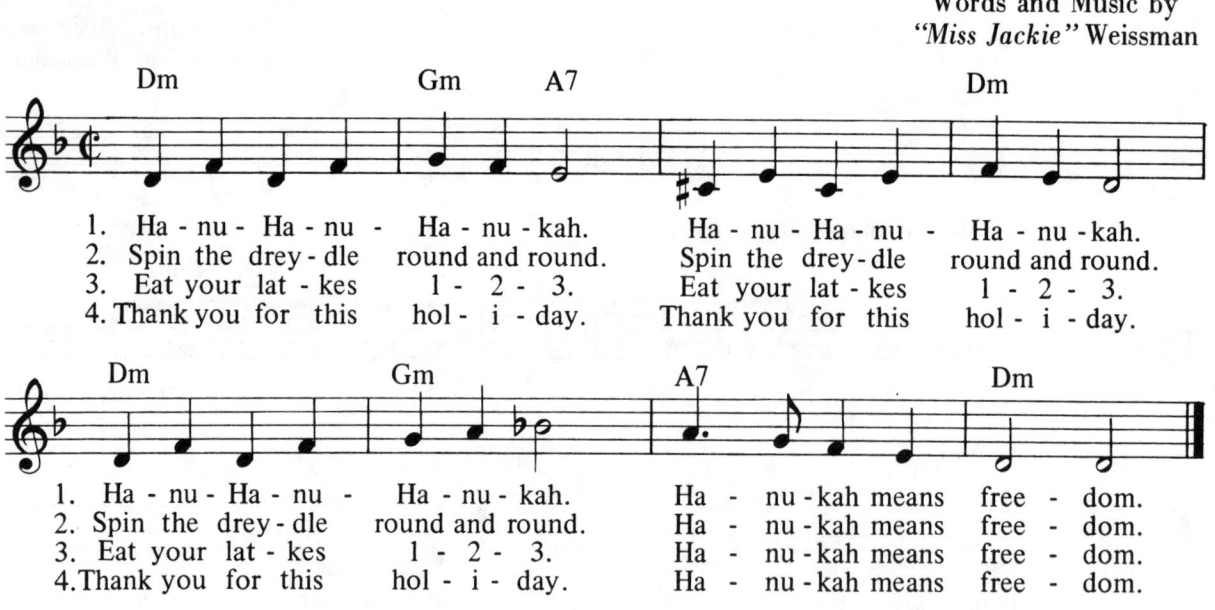

© 1982

ACTIVITIES

THERE are three acceptable spellings of Hanukah: Hanukah, Hannukah, and Chanukah.

THE HOLIDAY is a celebration of the defeat of the Syrian Army by Judah Maccabee in the year 165 B.C. This defeat gave the Jews freedom to worship as they believed and to rebuild their temple in Jerusalem. The holiday is meaningful to all people because it represents freedom.

DREIDLE—A spinning top with a Hebrew letter on each side. Children play a game using candy for money.

LATKES—Potato pancakes. These are traditionally eaten at Hanukah time. They are usually served with applesauce or sour cream.

THE FIRST three lines of each verse repeat the same words. The last line of all the verses says "Hanukah is freedom." Children can make up their own verses based on the information they have about the holiday.

NOTE: It is best to compare Hanukah to Thanksgiving, which is also a holiday of freedom.

TURKEY TALK

Words and Music by
"Miss Jackie" Weissman

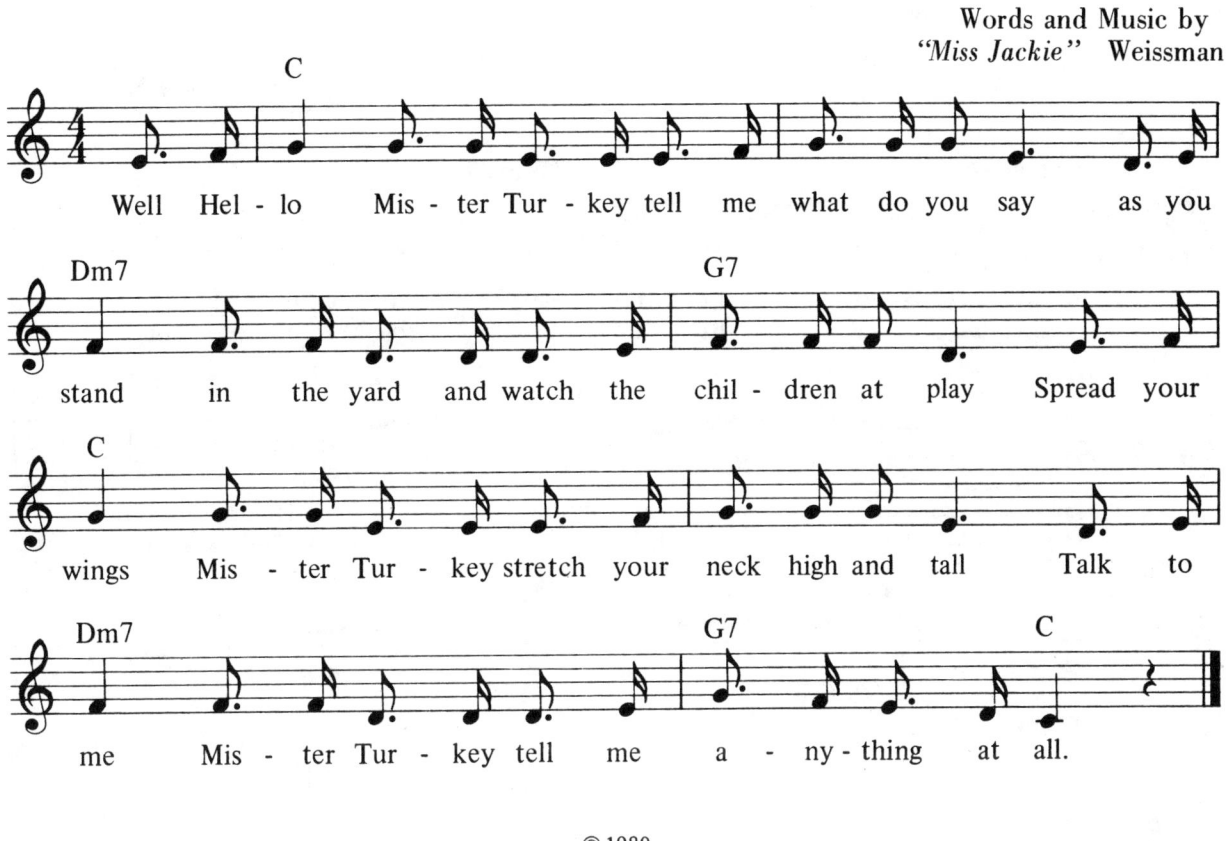

© 1980

THIS song gives children the opportunity to explore sound in many different ways. What does a turkey's voice sound like? Is it high, low, loud, soft, fast, or slow? How does a turkey say "hello"? How does a turkey say "I want to play"? Have the children talk to each other using "turkey talk."

LISTENING SKILLS—Tell the children a story. Every time they hear the word "turkey," they make "turkey talk."

DRAMATIC PLAY—Make turkey masks from paper bags or wear a turkey picture as you sing the song.

LANGUAGE—Make up a sentence and substitute one of the words with the word "turkey." Let the children guess what the substituted word is.

IDENTIFICATION—If possible, make a field trip to see a real turkey. Show pictures of turkeys and other kinds of birds. Discuss the ways that various birds fly.

GIVE

Words and Music by
"Miss Jackie" Weissman

© 1981

ACTIVITIES

"OUT OF the mouths of babes...." I asked a group of children what is the same about Thanksgiving and Christmas. They suggested that at Thanksgiving we give thanks for our wonderful country, give love to our families, and that the Indians gave help to the Pilgrims in planting. At Christmas we give gifts to our friends and family.

DISCUSSION—What kinds of things can you give to someone? To your parents? Grandparents? Your brother or sister? What can you give to a baby or a pet? Is it necessary to buy something in order to have something to give?

MUSIC—Sing this song while exchanging gifts, giving hugs, sitting in a circle and passing a toy from child to child.

ART—Cut pictures out of magazines that show people giving things to each other—hugs, love, gifts. Or cut out pictures of things you could give to another person. Paste the pictures in a book and give it to someone else.

CUT OUT construction letters—G, I, V, E—and paste them on a posterboard. Make lists of words that start with these sounds and print them under the proper letter.

LITTLE BETTY BLUE

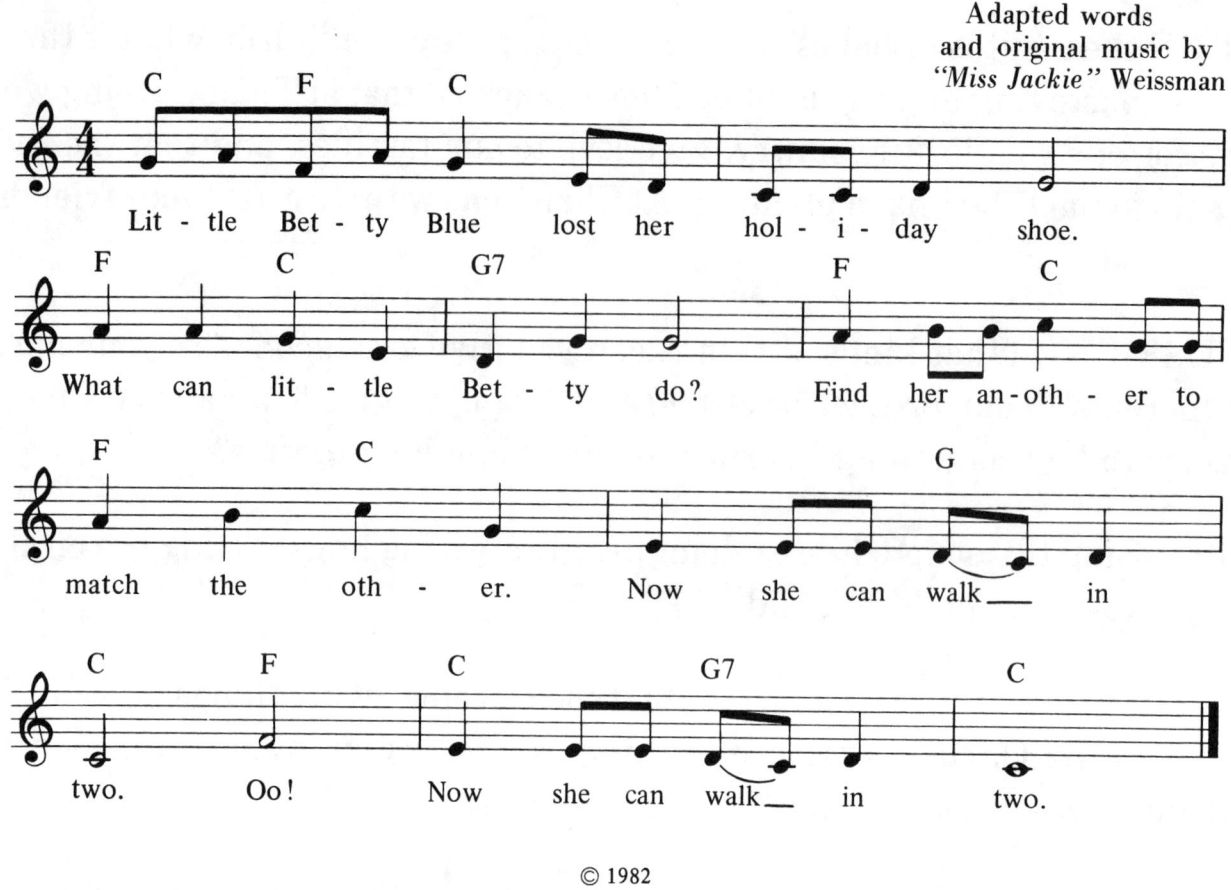

Adapted words and original music by "Miss Jackie" Weissman

© 1982

RHYMING WORDS AND RECOGNIZING COLORS—Change blue to a different color and let the children rhyme the color word: red/bed, black/sack, blue/shoe.

SELF CONCEPT—Change the name "Betty" to the name of the children in the class. Include everybody.

MATH GAME—As you sing the song, have a child put his or her shoes in a visible place. Then, another child. Now you can sing "now she can walk in four." Two more shoes and you can sing "now she can walk in six" and keep counting in twos. When all the children have their shoes in the pile, reverse the procedure and subtract by twos.

HOLIDAYS—What kind of shoes do you wear at holiday time? Are your "dress-up" shoes different from your school shoes? What kind of shoes did the Pilgrims wear? How about Santa Claus and his elves? Do animals wear shoes?

THE SNIGGLE SONG

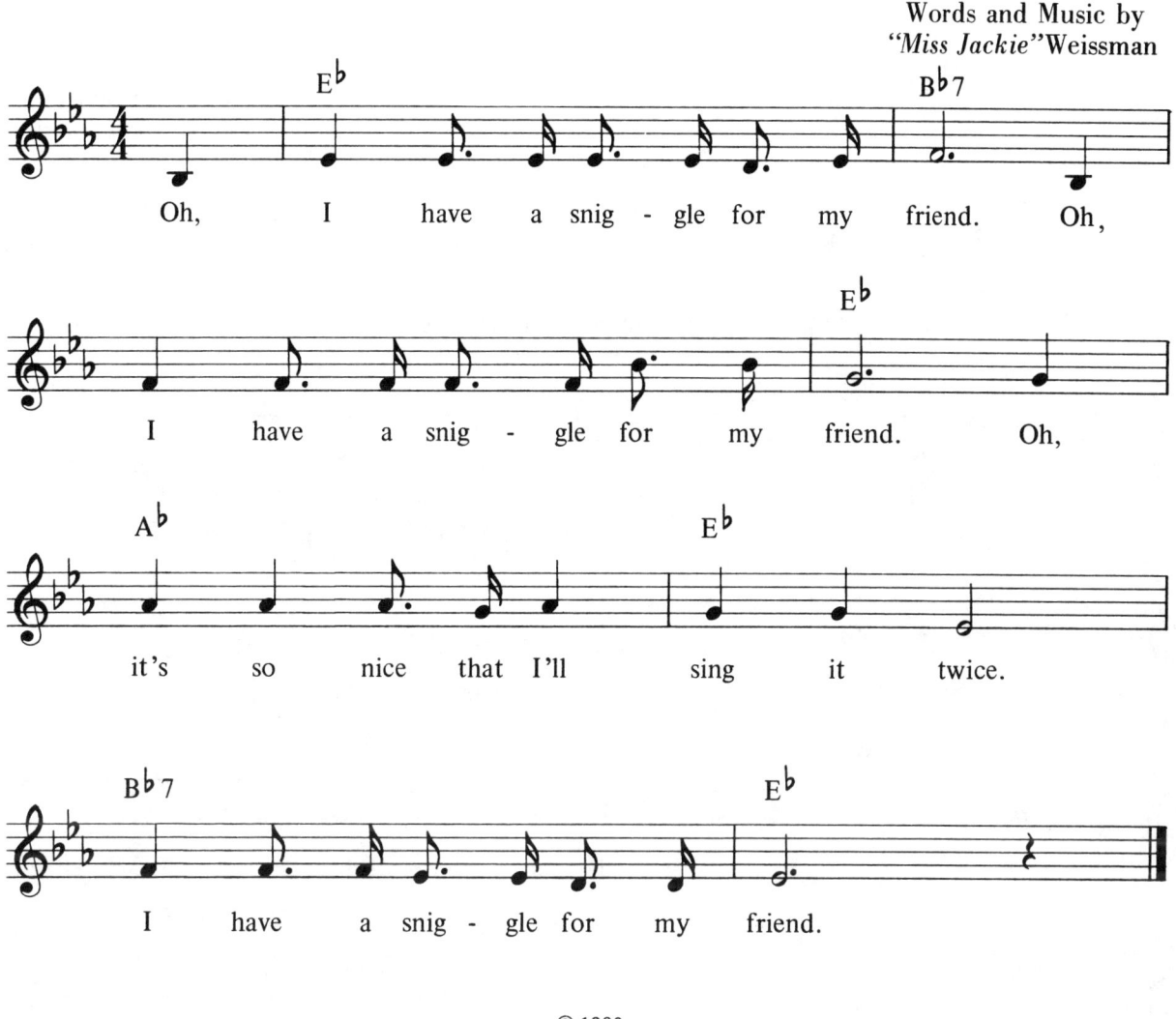

Words and Music by "Miss Jackie" Weissman

© 1980

THIS song is open-ended and, if carefully directed, can develop and encourage the creative process in young children.

SING the chorus, "Oh, I have a sniggle for my friend," and teach it to the children. Each time you sing a verse, follow with the chorus so that each child is participating.

BEWARE! Keep the sniggle without sex. As soon as you say "he" or "she," you put a limit on the sniggle's potential.

ASK THESE questions about the sniggle: Where does the sniggle live? What does the sniggle eat? What does the sniggle say? Sing the answers that the children give:

HAVE the children draw a sniggle. Collect the drawings and see how many different kinds of sniggles you collect. If you'd like to send me some sniggle pictures, I'd love it!!

NINE LITTLE REINDEER

Words and Music by
"Miss Jackie" Weissman

Peek - ing thru the win - dow what do I see, one lit - tle two lit - tle three lit - tle rein - deer.
Skip - ping thru the sky with a click - e - ty click, four lit - tle five lit - tle six lit - tle rein - deer.

Bet - ter go to bed. Bet - ter close my eyes. If I want a big sur - prise. Lis - ten to the roof top, what do I hear? Seven lit - tle eight lit - tle nine lit - tle rein - deer rein - deer.

© 1980

ACTIVITIES

WHY IS this song called "Nine Little Reindeer?" Read the portion from *A Visit from St. Nicholas* where the reindeer names are listed. Have the children count the names. Oops, only eight names! Someone will soon discover that Rudolph is missing!

SING the song and act out the parts. Cup your hands in front of your eyes and "peek." Raise a finger for each number as you count the reindeer. Cup your hand behind your ear to "listen." Have the children skip around the room on "skipping through the sky."

THE PENTATONIC melody of this song is gentle, soft, and flowing. It lends itself to bell-like sounds. Triangles, bells, and glockenspiels—any jingly instrument—can be played with this song. Give each child an instrument and have them play on the numbers.

IN ADDITION to the numbers, the key words in "Nine Little Reindeer" are "peeking," "listen," and "hear." Talk about things the children would like to peek through, listen to, or hear.

CLASSIFICATION—Pictures of animals with and without antlers can help the children learn to classify. A trip to the zoo to see the reindeer would be fun!

MOVEMENT—Have the children pretend to be reindeer. How do reindeer walk, hop, jump, prance, run? Let them pretend they are pulling Santa's sleigh.

MATH READINESS—Paste pictures of reindeer on cards and number the cards. Make two sets. The children pick a card from one set and match it with the same card from the other set.

GAME—Form a circle with nine children. They are the reindeer. Each reindeer comes to the center of the circle and, using a reindeer name, says "My name is _____ and here is my trick." Then the child does a reindeer trick. Make sure that each child in the class gets to have a turn.

GOING OUT TO PLAY

Words and Music by
"Miss Jackie" Weissman

Zip-per up my coat. Put my mit-tens on.
Scarf a-round my neck. Feet in-to my boots.
I am go-ing to play out - side.
It is snow-ing ev-ery-where. Bet-ter cov-er
up my hair. O-pen up the door. Step in-to the snow.
I am go-ing out-side. GOOD-BYE!

©1981

"GOING Out to Play" provides vocabulary for the children to act out each line. Have the children pantomime the actions in the song: zip up coats, put mittens on, etc. This song develops self concept and the importance of taking care of yourself. It is important for a young child to learn to dress properly for weather conditions.

LANGUAGE—Talk about the different ways to say "good-bye." You can wave good-bye, shake hands, hug. What other ways can you say good-bye? "See you later," "have a good day," or just plain "bye-bye" are a few. Let the children tell you different ways they say good-bye to different people: the mail carrier, the doctor, their parents, etc. Substitute the words when you sing the song. What's a fun way to say good-bye? "See you later, alligator." What are some more?

NO NO NO

Words and Music by
"Miss Jackie" Weissman

© 1980

THIS song is appropriate for babies as young as six months, and for children up to six years old. It can also be sung "yes, yes, yes."

WE OFTEN must say "no" to our children. They often say "no" to us. The danger in saying "no" is that the way in which it is said can arouse feelings of hostility in both parent and child. This song is a way to soften the concept of "no" while retaining its meaning.

SINGING this song is a non-threatening way to tell a child "no" and, at the same time, relieve tension in both adult and child.

SHAKE your head "no" when you sing the "no" part and nod your head "yes" when you sing the "yes" part.

WHEN you sing the "no" words, it's fun to shake your finger, stick out your tongue, or stamp your foot.

CAN YOU think of some actions for the "yes" part?

SING ABOUT MARTIN

Words and Music by
"Miss Jackie" Weissman

©1983

ACTIVITIES

"SING About Martin" is an echo song. Every sentence is echoed. The teacher sings a line and the children sing a line.

AFTER the children have learned the song, divide the class into two parts and have one part sing the first line, the other part sing the second line, etc. Divide the class in many different ways: by color of clothes, by color of eyes, by food preferences (cake vs. pie).

MARTIN Luther King Jr. was a great man. Why? What do we mean by caring? What do we mean by loving? The term "non-violence" may be too difficult for young children, but the concept of not fighting is certainly within their grasp.

THIS song has a gospel flavor and encourages clapping, stamping, snapping of fingers, etc. Try using rhythm instruments with a tambourine at the end of each line.

STAGE a pretend march across the room singing this song. Other songs to use are "This Land Is Your Land" and "God Bless America."

RIDE SALLY RIDE

Words and Music by
"Miss Jackie" Weissman

© 1983

ACTIVITIES

I FELT that the first woman astronaut was an historical event and deserved a special song.

CHILDREN are so turned on to space that this song provides a wonderful opportunity to talk about all kinds of work and male and female roles. I've met many a four-year-old who could not accept the fact that a woman could be a police officer or a firefighter. Now that a woman has been nominated for the vice presidency, it will be a little easier to make the point.

LET THE children pretend that they are in a space capsule. Do the countdown, and then sing the song.

THE SONG'S melody has a gentle, flowing feeling which lends itself to moving around the room while singing. It's best to let half of the children sing while the other half moves and then switch.

A NICE discussion about being proud of things can ensue. Ask the children what they have done that they were proud of. How do you act when you are proud? How do you hold your body? What do you do with your hands?

COMPARING things that fly is a nice activity to follow this song. Birds, insects, planes, kites. Try to move like all of these things.

HOORAY FOR MR. LINCOLN

Words and Music by
"Miss Jackie" Weissman

© 1981

ACTIVITIES

THIS song leads to much discussion and has many important vocabulary words: Lincoln, Washington, celebrate, country, American, red, white, and blue. Have the children make their own American flags. Let them wave their flags while marching around the room singing the song.

STUDY the American flag. Count the stars. Why are there 50? Look at the flags of other countries. Are they similar to our flag? Do they have the same colors? What do the colors mean?

SAY "hip hip hooray" two times. On the third time say only "hip hip" and on the word "hooray" start singing the song.

EACH time you sing the word "hooray," lead the children in a different action such as stamping feet, clapping hands, and so on.

MARCH with your feet. March with your hands (fingers together, palms in). March with your fingers.

HAVE a red, white, and blue day. Wear those colors. Use only red, white, and blue crayons or paints for the day. Have red, white, and blue treats.

LOOK MA! NO CAVITIES

Words and Music by
"Miss Jackie" Weissman

© 1983

ACTIVITIES

THIS song has lots of opportunities to teach about good health and good nutrition.

WHILE you are singing the song, have the children learn the proper way to brush their teeth. Most dentists recommend the "up-and-down" method. And brushing the gums is important.

ON THE words "I love to eat apples," let the children substitute their own words about foods that are good for their teeth.

DENTISTS tell us that flossing the teeth is important for good dental health, so let the children pretend to be flossing while singing the song.

PERHAPS your local dentist would lend you a model of a tooth to use when singing this song.

DISCUSS teeth. How many teeth does a person have? What are different kinds of teeth (molars, front teeth, eye teeth, etc.)? What is a cavity? How can we avoid cavities?

TALK about the teeth of animals. How do animals keep their teeth clean without brushing or flossing?

FOR FUN, sing the song in a cat voice, a duck voice, a lion voice.

GROUNDHOG

Words and Music by
"Miss Jackie" Weissman

1. Ground-hog Ground-hog come on out and play. It's a beau-ti-ful beau-ti-ful Feb-ru-a-ry day. The sun is shin-ing and the sky is blue. Won't you come on out? I want to play with you.

2. Ground-hog Ground-hog come on out and play. It's a gloo-my gloo-my Feb-ru-a-ry day. The air feels chil-ly and the sky is gray. Won't you come on out? I want to play to-day.

© 1980

ACTIVITIES

"GROUNDHOG" is a good song for playacting. The children learn about Groundhog Day by pretending to be a groundhog. Sing the first verse of the song, then play this game. The groundhog comes out of his hole, looks around, sees his shadow, and cries, "Oh, no, six more weeks of winter." For the second part of the game, sing the second part of the song. Then the groundhog comes out of his hole and, not seeing his shadow, exclaims, "Oh, I'm so happy. I don't see my shadow."

CREATIVE EXPRESSION—Show the children pictures of groundhogs. Talk about where groundhogs live, how they move, what sounds they make. Let the children talk to one another in a groundhog voice. Talk about other animals that live in the ground. Moles and rabbits are two good examples. What do they eat?

GO OUTSIDE and let the children observe their shadows. Make your shadows do different things. Jump up and down, make your shadow very small, make it very big.

BACK in the classroom, shine a light against a white background. Let the children make shadows on the screen using their bodies and hands.

UNITED

Words and Music by
"Miss Jackie" Weissman

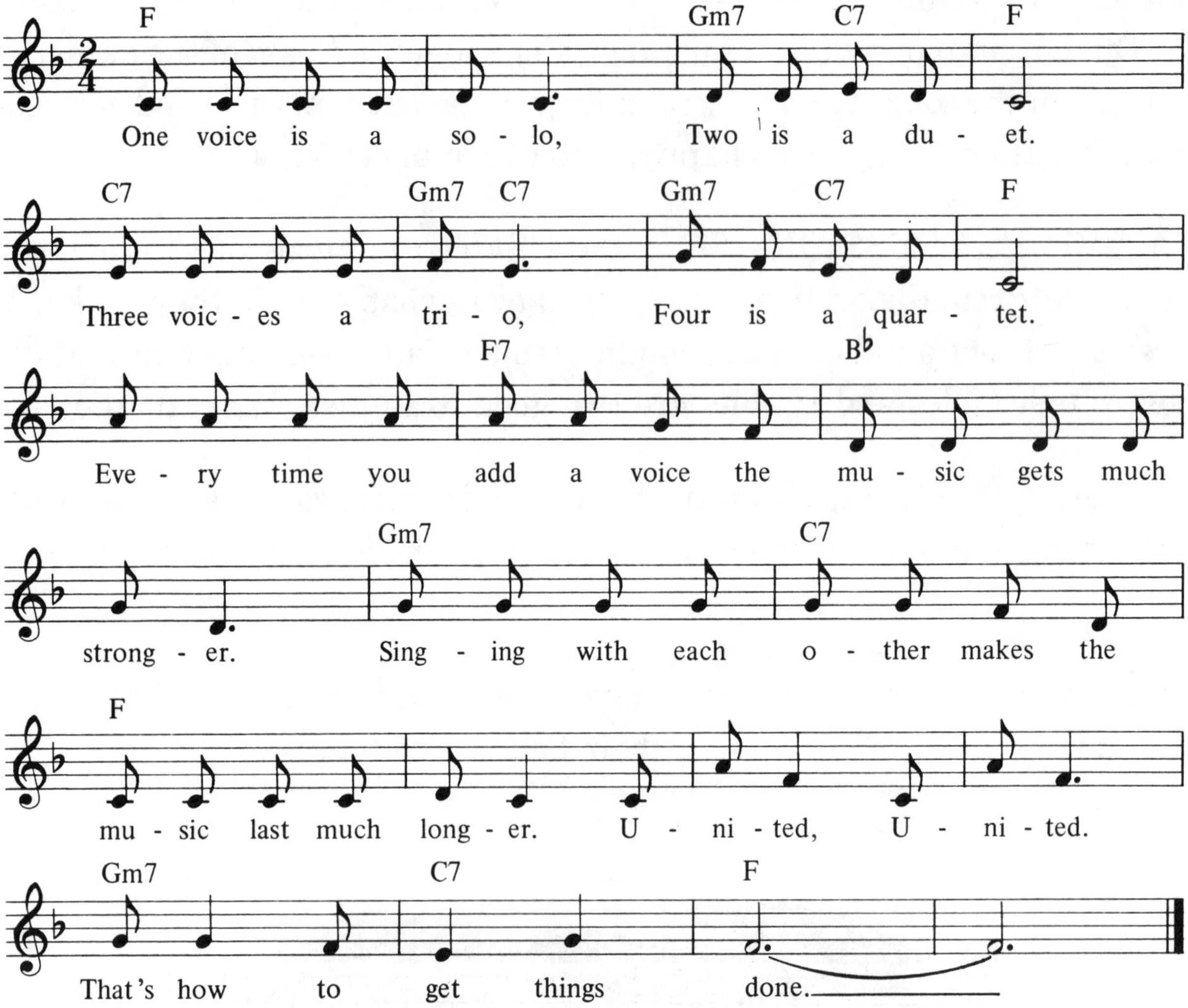

One voice is a so - lo, Two is a du - et.
Three voic - es a tri - o, Four is a quar - tet.
Eve - ry time you add a voice the mu - sic gets much
strong - er. Sing - ing with each o - ther makes the
mu - sic last much long - er. U - ni - ted, U - ni - ted.
That's how to get things done.

©1983

ACTIVITIES

THIS song was inspired by United Nations Day. It provides an opportunity to understand how working together can solve problems. The old adage "Two heads are better than one" applies here.

MUSICAL VOCABULARY—Solo, duet, trio, quartet. After the children have learned the song, begin again, first with one voice, then two, then three, then four, following the words of the song.

MORE VOCABULARY—Solo means one. What other words mean one? (Single, etc.) Duet means two. What other words mean two? (Pair, etc.)

DISCUSSION—Why are some jobs easier when more than one person helps? Can you ride a teeter-totter alone? Is cleaning up the room easier alone or together?

IF THE class is mature enough, you could discuss the United Nations: how it works, what countries belong to it, that its purpose is to promote peace and understanding among nations.

GOOD-BYE WINTER, HELLO SPRING

ACTIVITIES

THIS song is meant to encourage children to use their senses in detecting the changes in nature that occur in the spring. Have the children dramatize the words "shh," "look," "ooh" (rhymes with "new"), and "all."

SCIENCE—Take a nature walk with the class, observing the various changes that happen in the spring. See snow melting, flowers peeping, and trees beginning to awake from their winter sleep. Listen to the wind whistling, the birds singing. Take along a magnifying glass for closer looks.

GAME—Play a March wind game. Let the children form a circle and pretend they are trees. Each child can be a different kind of tree. One child is the wind. The wind rushes through the trees, making a wind sound. When teacher gives a signal, the wind stops and trades places with a tree. The tree child then becomes the wind.

CREATIVE DRAMATICS—Find pictures of flowers peeping, birds singing, noses stinging, snow melting, and trees breathing as they begin to blossom. Mount the pictures on oak tags. Mix the pictures up and see if the child can put them in the same order as they appear in the song. Have the children act out the song, using the pictures for a guide.

WIND DISCUSSION—Can you see the wind? How does the wind blow different things differently? How does a flag react to the wind compared to leaves of grass? Have the children pretend to be blown about by the wind.

KING OF THE JUNGLE

Words and Music by
"Miss Jackie" Weissman

Ho Ho Ho I'm the King of the jun-gle. Ho Ho Ho I'm the ru-ler of the crowd. Ho Ho Ho I'm the King of the jun-gle. Ho Ho Ho I can ROAR scar-y loud. Do what I tell you. Do what I say or I'll ROAR and I'll ROAR and I'll fright-en you a-way.

© 1980

ACTIVITIES

LITTLE children are not often in a power position. "King of the Jungle" is a creative dramatics song that allows children to vent feelings *and* to be in a power position. This is important to a child's development.

HAVE the children play rhythm instruments on the "ho, ho, ho" parts.

ON THE "roar" parts, have the children make the sound rather than say the word.

DURING "do what I tell you and do what I say" have them shake their index fingers at one another.

CREATIVE DRAMATICS—Have the children sing the song in a low voice "like a lion."

DISCUSSION—Show the children pictures of lions. Talk about the cat family; their strength, their speed, why lions are called kings of the jungle.

MOVEMENT—Talk about different kinds of animals. Move around the room like a lion, a tiger, an elephant, a monkey.

CLASSIFICATION—Look at pictures of animals that belong to the cat family. What is it about these animals that makes them similar? Fur, feet, whiskers? Compare them to human families. Do they care for their young in the same way?

GAME—Cut out pictures of the feet of different animals. Have the children identify the animals by their feet.

LISTENING—Divide the class into two parts. One part sings "ho, ho, ho" and the other part sings the rest of the line. Everyone sings the "do" part.

EASTER BUNNY

Words and Music by
"Miss Jackie" Weissman

2nd Verse:

If I were a bunny,
I'd tell you what I'd say,
"Howdy, folks, Hello to you
And Happy Easter Day."

Hoppin' along . . . . *etc.*

©1980

ACTIVITIES

SING the song using body movement or finger play. You can hop with your feet, your fingers, your head, your elbow, or other parts of your body. Clap hands or snap fingers during the chorus. In the second verse, first say "Howdy" and "Hello." Then say hello in other languages: "Buenos dias," "Guten tag," and "Top o' the morning."

CREATIVE MOVEMENT—Talk about how bunnies hop. Have the children pretend they are bunnies hopping about. Have them hop fast, slow, high, bumpy. Give them vocabulary words related to hopping: graceful, jerky, dreamy, quick.

SPATIAL RELATIONS—Find a large open box that the children can hop into. Play a game of hopping to learn spatial relationships. Hop into the box; hop out of the box; hop to the side of the box; hop over the box; hop under the box.

NUTRITION—What do rabbits eat? Where do they find their food? Do they cook it?

CREATIVITY—The verses of the song tell what the bunny will do and say. Create more verses about what the bunny will touch, smell, hear and see.

OBSERVATION—If possible, bring a small bunny to the classroom. Let the children observe it and discuss its actions.

DIDDLE DIDDLE DUMPLING

Adapted words and original music by *"Miss Jackie"* Weissman

© 1982

ACTIVITIES

THE WORDS "Diddle, Diddle, Dumpling" are fun to say and to sing. Do anyone's parents call their child "dumpling" as a term of affection? What *do* the children's parents call them? What do they call one another? There will be a lot of laughing as the class discusses this.

SOUNDS—Sing the song with different beginning sounds. Try a "b" sound: "biddle, biddle, bumpling." Or a "z" sound: "ziddle, ziddle, zumpling." Have the class discuss other beginning sounds.

MUSICAL GAME—Divide the class into two parts. Have them sing:

PART 1: Diddle, diddle, dumpling, dumpling, dumpling.
PART 2: Diddle, diddle, dumpling. My son John.
PART 1: Went to bed with his stockings, stockings,
PART 2: Went to bed with his stockings on.
PART 1: One (count of 4)
PART 2: One shoe off.
PART 1: One (count of 4)
PART 2: One shoe on.
PART 1: Diddle, diddle, dumpling. Diddle, diddle, dumpling.
PART 2: Diddle, diddle, dumpling.
ALL: MY SON JOHN!!

WHEN the children have learned the two parts, introduce rhythm instruments, clapping or stamping. Let one part of the class sing with voices; let the other part "sing" with instruments. Change parts.

NAMES—Change the name "John" to the names of children in the class. This might be a wonderful way to get acquainted on the first day of school.

DISCUSSION—Talk about what you wear to bed. Do you wear your stockings? Do you take stuffed animals to bed?

WHISTLING COWHAND

Words and Music by
"Miss Jackie" Weissman

Oh, a cow {hand's/girl's} life is a might-y fine life: Work-ing all the day, sleep-ing all the night. If I do my chores or I ride my horse, I can al-ways hum__ a song.

Refrain (to whistle)*

*Children can make up their own whistling refrain:
if you use "hum", kids hum; if you use "sing", kids go "la, la, la".

© 1982

THIS song can be acted out line by line.

A DISCUSSION of the word "chores" can ensue with the children telling of the "chores" they have to do.

ON THE refrain, the children can do many things. They can make different kinds of mouth sounds, stamp feet, swing hips or move with a partner.

THE REFRAIN is also excellent for rhythm instruments. Sticks, tone blocks and sand blocks sound particularly nice.

BABY MOSES

Words and Music by
"Miss Jackie" Weissman

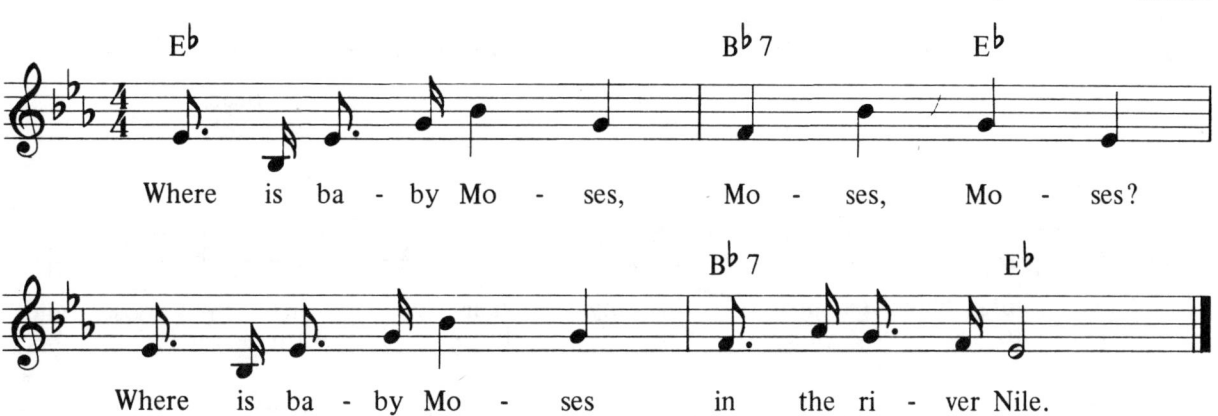

Where is ba-by Mo-ses, Mo-ses, Mo-ses?
Where is ba-by Mo-ses in the ri-ver Nile.

He is in a basket *(3x)*
The princess she is swimming *(3x)*
She finds the baby Moses. *(3x)*

© 1970

THIS song was originally written for three- and four-year-olds. If you have older children, you can extend the story of Moses by making up more verses.

EACH verse has an action:

WHERE'S the baby Moses?—Cup hands over eyes as if you are looking for someone.

HE IS in a basket—Rock arms as if you are holding a baby.

THE PRINCESS she is swimming—Children pretend they are swimming.

SHE FINDS the baby Moses—Pick up the baby and hold it close.

HAVE the children each bring a doll or stuffed animal to class. Sing and act out the song with the dolls.

BABY BEAR'S CHICKEN POX

Words and Music by
"Miss Jackie" Weissman

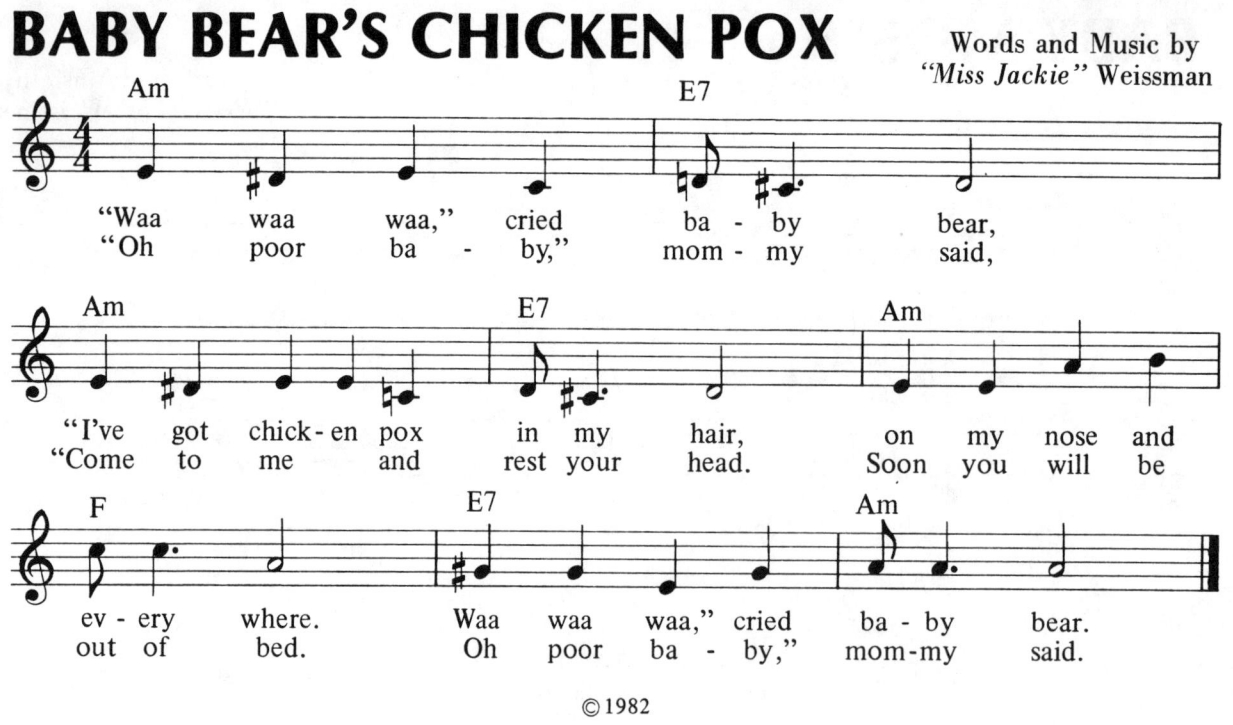

"Waa waa waa," cried ba-by bear,
"Oh poor ba-by," mom-my said,
"I've got chick-en pox in my hair, on my nose and ev-ery where. Waa waa waa," cried ba-by bear.
"Come to me and rest your head. Soon you will be out of bed. Oh poor ba-by," mom-my said.

©1982

LEARNING can be fun! This song provides a creative dramatic experience combined with humor and nurturing. Make up actions to go with the song. Rub eyes for the "waa waa waa" part. Substitute mommy with daddy or grandma.

THE PARTS, mommy and baby, can be sung in different voices. The song has a nice syncopated feel. Use rhythm instruments and body movement to express the rhythm.

DISCUSSION—Do you ever get sick? How does it feel? Who takes care of you?

ART—Draw a bear with chicken pox or a monkey with mumps. Have the children think of different animals and how they would look with different sicknesses.

CREATIVE PLAY—Imagine how a bear would sound laughing; how a frog would cry. Make up a chicken voice.

SCIENCE—Where do bears live? Are there different kinds of bears? What do they have in common? How are they different?

LANGUAGE—What would you do if your baby had the chicken pox? Develop vocabulary that expresses nurturing.

WATER IN THE RAIN CLOUDS

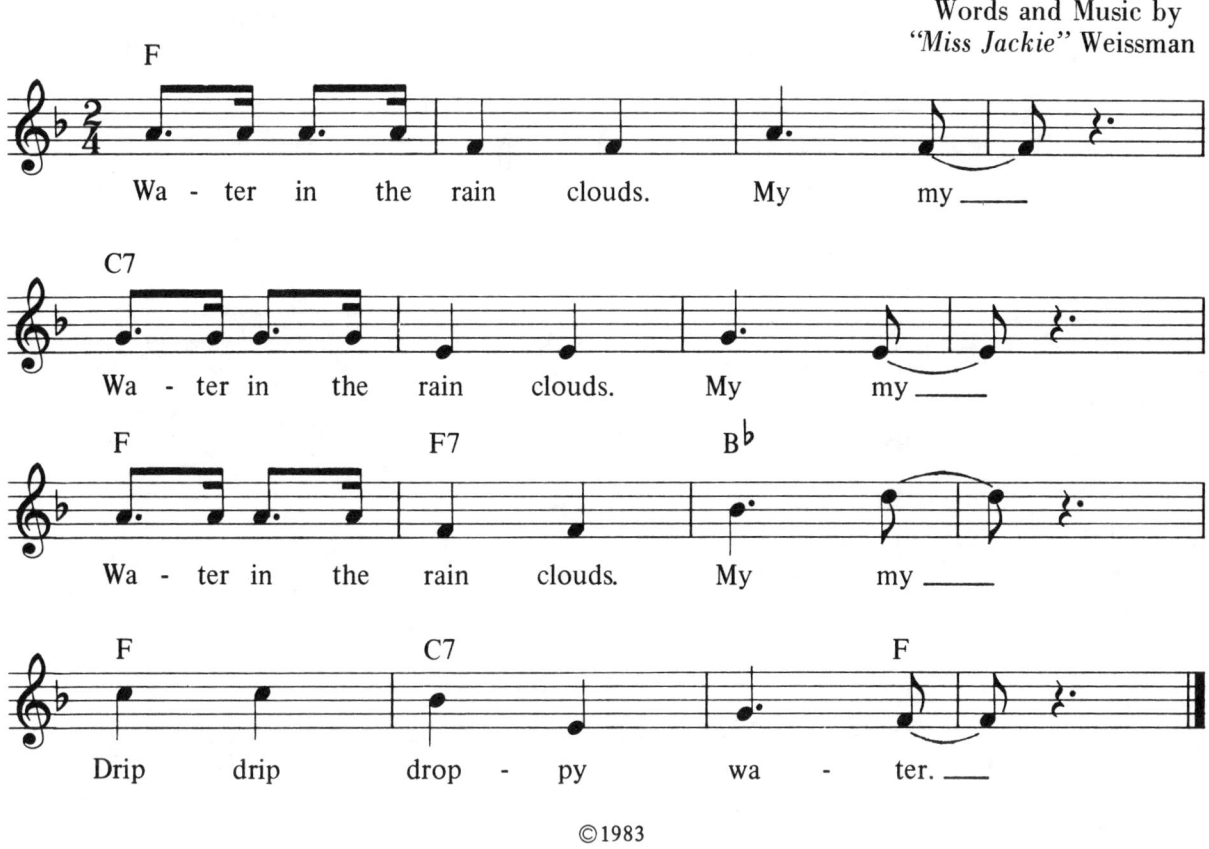

WATER is one of our most valuable natural resources. This song will help young children become more aware of all the many aspects of water and the many ways we use water.

THE WORDS "my my" that appear at the end of each verse can be changed by the children: "Oh yes," "hurrah," etc.

THE LAST line, "Splish splish splashy water," can be changed to fit whatever you are singing about in the particular verse. For example, "Water in the rain clouds" could be "drip drip drippy water." Water in the faucet could be "drink drink drinky water."

A POEM to accompany this song is, "Rain, Rain, Go Away." An appropriate book would be "A Child's Garden of Verses" by Robert Louis Stevenson.

TODAY IS MAY

THE SYNCOPATION of this song lends itself very nicely to the use of rhythm instruments. Triangles, drums, bells, and sticks can be used together or separately to play the last note of each line, which is the ideal place to play them.

VARY the way the class sings the song. One way would be to have one child sing "sing a song" and the rest of the class sing "today is May."

SOME of the children may not know the word "celebrate," so explain the word to the whole class. Talk about things we celebrate: birthdays, holidays, etc. Why would we celebrate a lovely day? Why do people in different parts of the world celebrate on different days?

FINALLY—Take the class outside, sing the song, and celebrate a lovely day!

CONVERSATION WITH A TREE

Words and Music by
"Miss Jackie" Weissman

©1983

THIS song will help children become aware of things that we get from trees. Shade, fruit, nuts, beauty, etc.

EACH time that you sing the song, you can guide the questioning to teach the concept about trees that you are trying to get across. For example, you want the children to know about the different kinds of trees that bear fruit. First you would talk about them so that they would have some vocabulary to work with. Then one child can be the tree. When you sing the part, "What's your name?" the child will answer, "I'm a plum." Then your questioning can continue with many things: Where do you live? Are you tall? Do you have green leaves? The possibilities are endless.

THE OPEN endedness of this song makes it possible for children to learn about any kind of tree. Other activities that can accompany this song are taking a nature walk and identifying trees, smelling leaves and becoming aware of their aroma, sitting under a tree and enjoying its shade and beauty.

SINGING this song will help children internalize an appreciation of the natural world that surrounds them.

ACTIVITIES

THIS song is meant to be acted out. Children love to "wiggle" and "squiggle" like worms. Their imaginations will tell them how to "wiggle" and "squiggle." They can use their whole bodies to be the worms or just parts of their bodies, their fingers or toes, for example.

VOCABULARY DEVELOPMENT—Discuss different kinds of worms. Describe them by length, color, width, and texture. What other creatures remind you of worms?

BEGINNING SOUNDS—Cut out large letters—W, O, R, M—from construction paper. Paste each letter on a separate piece of poster board. Let the children look through magazines and find things that begin with these letters.

ART—Make a worm picture. Glue thick white string on construction paper.

SCIENCE—Visit a worm farm if you have one in your area. Why are worms good for the earth? Do you know that worms are used for many things, including food? Believe it or not! Watch birds dig for worms and feed them to their young. This can be done in the schoolyard, especially after a heavy rainfall.

WHAT are some things that look like worms? Spaghetti, pipe cleaners . . . What else?

OLD MOTHER HUBBARD

Original music and adaptation by
"Miss Jackie" Weissman

Old Mother Hubbard, she went to the cupboard, to get her poor dog a bone. When she got there, the cupboard was bare, so her poor dog had none. BOO HOO HOO BOO HOO HOO HOO HOO. When she got there, the cupboard was bare. So her poor dog had none. HAD NONE. *(Shout)*

© 1982

ACTIVITIES

THIS song gives children a chance to "spread their creative wings." The verses can be logical or silly or dramatic. Recite the poem to the children. Many of them will probably be familiar with it. When you have taught all the children the poem, then sing the melody. Add the crying part and the last part. Children like to shout the tag ending.

NOW BEGIN the substitutions: "She went to the cupboard to get her poor dog a ..." and let the children fill in. Example: dress, hat, pizza. Then substitute the animals: "She went to the cupboard to get her poor _____ a _____." Example: giraffe a cake, hippopotamus a banana. See what fun you'll have with this one!

CREATIVE DRAMATICS—On the "boo-hoo" part, have the children cry like the animal they are singing about. How does a dog cry? How about a duck?

CREATIVITY—Make two piles of pictures, one of animals and one of foods. Let a child pick an animal and a food (eyes closed, please). Whatever the animal and the food are, use them in the song: "Went to the cupboard to get her poor giraffe some meatballs," "her bumblebee some green beans," etc.

SING the song in a different kinds of voices: happy, sad, fast, slow. Make up movement or actions to go with the song. Remember, using movement and music together exercises both sides of the brain.

PETER PIPER

Words Traditional
Original Music by *"Miss Jackie"* Weissman

©1982

TONGUE twisters are fun. Young children who are just learning to speak and to read love them because it gives them a chance to have fun with words.

SING the song slowly the first time through. Then a little faster. Then a little faster. Then a lot faster, etc. Another nice thing is to raise the key one-half step each time you sing the song, again going a little faster each time.

WHAT are some other tongue twisters? Make up some new ones in class. Take the names of the children and make tongue twisters: Johnny jumped on Jerry in June. Silly Sally saw the salty soup. Mary made a marshmallow malt.

RHYTHM—Add hand and body movement:

```
Peter  Piper  picked a peck of picked    peppers.
CLAP CLAP CLAP   CLAP   STAMP STAMP STAMP STAMP
A peck of pickled peppers Peter Piper picked.
ST    ST    ST  ST F   F   F        F
```

CLAP—Clap hands together.
STAMP—Stamp feet.
ST—Slap thighs.
F—Make a fist with each hand and hit them together.

LITTLE MISS MUFFET

Adapted words and music by "Miss Jackie" Weissman

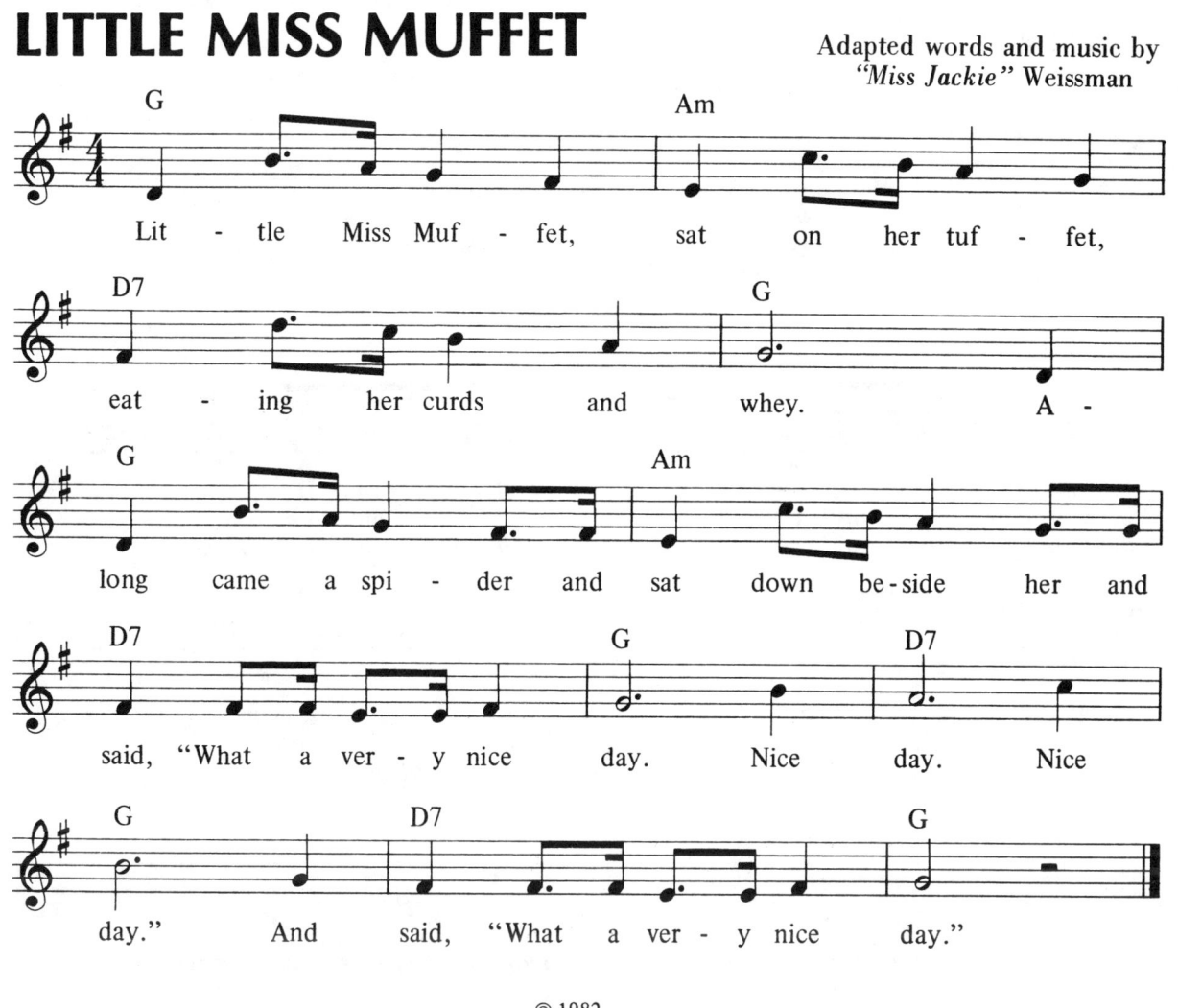

© 1982

THE ORIGINAL words of this nursery rhyme teach a message that is no longer applicable to today's society—that little girls are afraid of spiders and that spiders are always "bad."

THIS is a more open-ended version of the song. What else could the spider have said to Little Miss Muffet? He could have said, "It's a good day to play," or "What have you got to say?" Let the children complete the idea. The words don't have to rhyme. (One response I've had was, "The spider said, 'Let's go play PAC-MAN!'")

WHAT or who else could have sat down next to Little Miss Muffet? See what creative ideas the children will have about this.

VOCABULARY—What are curds and whey? Where do milk and cheese come from? What is a tuffet? (It's a small stool.)

CREATIVE DRAMATICS—While the class is singing, two of the children could act out the parts.

RAIN

Words and Music by
"Miss Jackie" Weissman

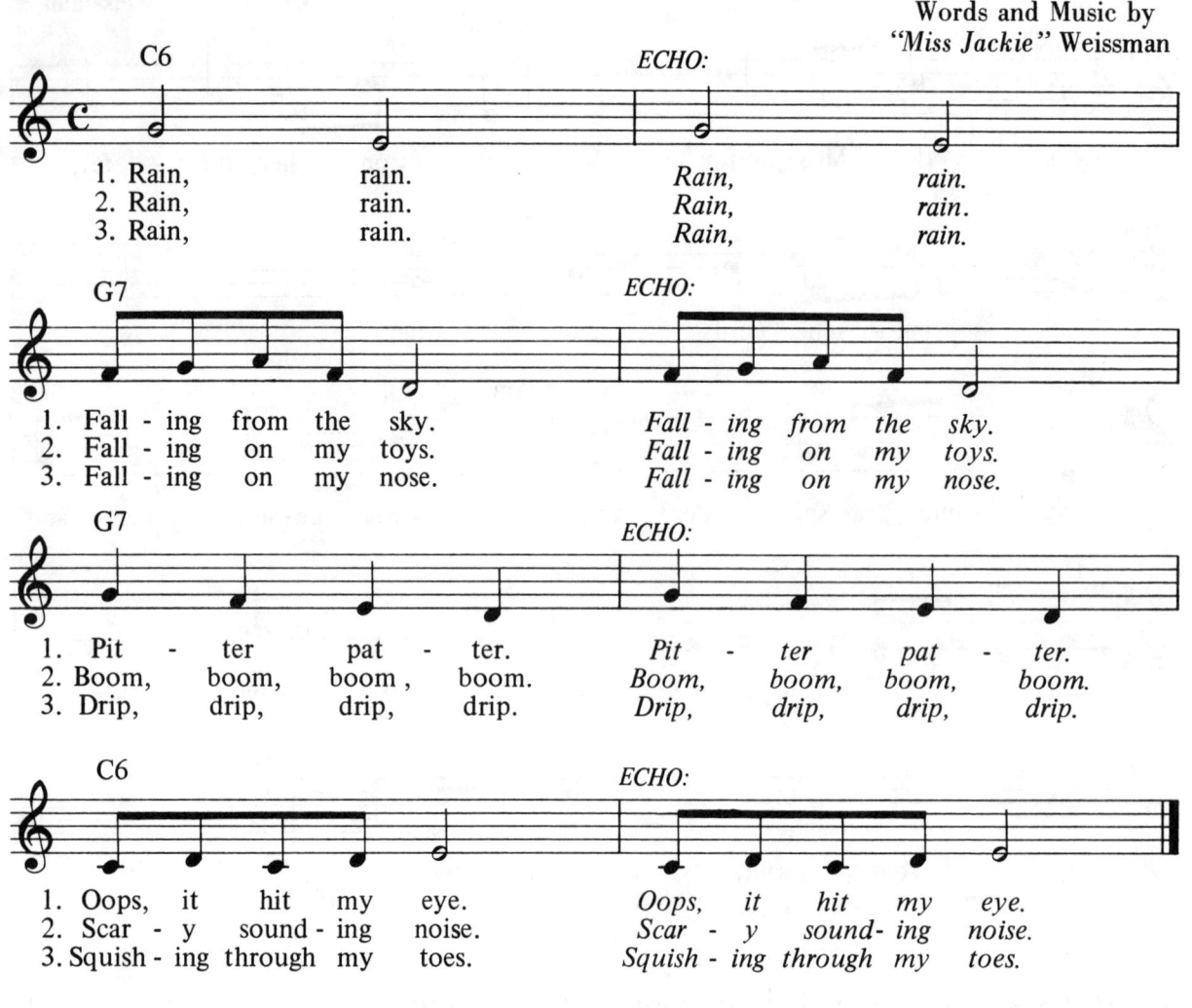

© 1982

MUSIC, language and movement come from different parts of the brain. It is important that children use both sides of their brains. By combining movement with language or music, you are using both sides.

FIRST of all, teach the song to the children. This is a call and response song. The teacher sings one line and the children echo the line.

AFTER the children have learned the song, add rhythm instruments and body movement for accompaniment: snap fingers, tap toes, shake hips, tap sticks, hit a drum.

HAVE a discussion about rain. Where does it come from? What are thunder and lightning? Are they scary?

DOES rain ever hit you in the eye? Does it hurt? Can it harm you?

HEY DIDDLE, DIDDLE

Words Traditional
Music by *"Miss Jackie"* Weissman

©1983

THE MUSIC to HDD has a blues-rock feeling. Clapping or snapping fingers makes a nice accompaniment. Perhaps you could bring in an older child to play drums behind the song. It would be very effective.

THIS SONG stimulates a lot of imagery and acting out the parts is great fun. You would need a cow playing a fiddle, a moon, dog, dish and spoon.

DISCUSS the word "sport." Differentiate from the meaning of sports as the children know them. Think of synonyms for "sport" such as silliness, fun, etc.

CREATING stories or poetry can be influenced by this song. Give the children three things to think about. An animal, an instrument that the animal is playing and the place that the animal is playing the instrument. For example, a dog playing a trumpet in the band. A lizard playing the drums on the roof. Follow an activity like this with an art project.

INDEX BY FIRST LINES

Aloha, Aloha, Aloha Means Hello 9
Animals Are My Friends 19
Black Cat, Black Cat, What Do You Think of That, Scat! 14
A Cowhand's Life Is a Mighty Fine Life 50
Diddle, Diddle, Dumpling, Dumpling, Dumpling 48
Everybody Quiet, Don't Make a Peep 16
Every Single Morning and Every Single Night 36
Give a Little Help to Your Neighbor 22
Groundhog, Groundhog, Come On Out and Play 38
H A L L O HO HO Double U E E EH EH N 15
Hanu- Hanu- Hanukah 20
Hello, Hello, You Are Beautiful 55
Hello Mr. Turkey, Tell Me What Do You Say? 21
Hey, Diddle, Diddle, the Cat and the Fiddle 63
I Have a Sniggle for My Friend 25
Ho, Ho, Ho, I'm the King of the Jungle 44
Hooray for Mr. Lincoln, Hooray for Mr. Washington 34
If I Were a Bunny, I'll Tell You What I'd Do 46
I'm a Fur Fur Furry Squirrel 12
Little Betty Blue Lost Her Holiday Shoe 24
Little Miss Muffet Sat on Her Tuffet 61
No, No, No, I Like to Say No 29
Old Mother Hubbard, She Went to the Cupboard 58
One Voice Is a Solo, Two Is a Duet 40
Peeking Through the Window, What Do I See 26
Peter Piper Picked a Peck of Pickled Peppers 60
Picking the Trash Up off the Street 10

Rain, Rain, Rain, Rain, Falling from the Sky 62

Ride, Sally, Ride. Spread Your Wings and Fly to the Sky 32

Roses Are Red, Violets Are Blue 8

Shh! The Grass Is Sleeping. Look a Flower's Peeping 42

Sing About Martin, Sing About Martin 30

Sing a Song, Sing a Song of September 6

Sing a Song, Today Is May 53

Waa, Waa, Waa, Cried Baby Bear 52

Water in the Rain Clouds, My, My 53

What Can I Do? What Will Make Me Smile? 18

Where Is Baby Moses, Moses, Moses? 51

Worms, Worms, Worms, Crawling in the Ground 56

Zipper Up My Coat, Put My Mittens On 28

About Miss Jackie

Jackie Weissman, better known as "Miss Jackie" to thousands of teachers, parents, and children throughout the U.S.A. and Canada, is a children's concert artist, composer, educator, consultant, national columnist, recording artist and TV personality.

She is an Adjunct Instructor in Early Childhood for Emporia State University and a monthly contributor to *The Instructor* magazine. Most of the songs in *Sniggles, Squirrels, and Chicken Pox* were originally published in *The Instructor*.

Miss Jackie is also the publisher of *Early Childhood Music* newsletter, a parent-teacher aid in the field of early childhood education.

The songs in *Sniggles, Squirrels, and Chicken Pox* are also available on an LP record or cassette tape.

For a complete catalog of other Miss Jackie materials write:

Miss Jackie Music Company
Dept. SSC
10001 El Monte
Overland Park, Kansas 66207

Books
Hello Rhythm
Hello Sound
All About Me
Let's Be Friends
Songs to Sing with Babies

Records and Tapes
Lollipops and Spaghetti
Peanut Butter, Tarzan, and Roosters
Sing Around the World
Hello Rhythm
Sing a Jewish Song
Let's Be Friends
All About Me
Songs to Sing with Babies
I'm a Headstart Kid
State Songs: Kansas, Iowa, Wisconsin, Missouri

NOTES

NOTES

NOTES

NOTES

NOTES

NOTES